AF472391

The "Joy" of Smoking

Raymond Stone

ISBN: 978-1-4834-0524-7 (sc)
ISBN: 978-1-4834-0523-0 (e)

Lulu Publishing Services rev. date: 12/10/2013

To my beautiful 'smoke-free' wife Karen, and my wonderful daughters Susan, Cathee and Lisa

Non-smoking evangelists are a huge pain in the butt. I have been a non-smoker many times. My most recent venture into the ranks of the smoke-free was in nineteen eighty-five. I'm not one of those holier-than-thou political/social-correctoid evangelists who insist that the rest of the world must 'see the light' and butt out. This is total insanity, and even though I don't smoke, I defend everyone's right to freedom of choice. Having said that, I agree that smoking kills. Anyone who smokes should seriously consider quitting. **That's the end of my sermon.** The rest of the book is devoted to providing interesting experiences, techniques and examples of how to quit the weed, as well as a few (hopefully) humorous stories and gags about our love/hate relationship with tobacco. Light up and enjoy.

Special thanks to: My wife Karen, Dave Brown, George Powell, Les McLaughlin, Lowell Green, Dr. Peter Gott, Ian Nicholson, Geoff Norquay, Bob Mellor, Bert Plimer, John Windich, and many, many other friends.

Acknowledgements

I would like to thank the thousands of smokers who have inspired me to quit smoking and remain smoke-free. With their incessant hacking, coughing, wheezing, spitting, snorting, barking, choking, gagging, and convulsing, they remain a constant reminder of what a stinky, stupid, messy, incon-venient, expensive, tedious, tiresome, noxious, annoying, bothersome, dirty, inconsiderate habit smoking actually is. They are a true inspiration.

R.P.S.

Chapter 1

I'm not going to lie to you.

It's damned hard to quit smoking. I know, because I did it about ten times before finally giving up the weed forever in March, 1985. I'll never forget the date, because it was while we were on vacation in Cuba, and it was a weird case of serendipity. I was sitting under a tree on the patio between the beach and the Hotel Internacional, enjoying the 80 degree sunshine, the fresh air and a general feeling of well- being, when I decided to light up a cigarette. I fished the half pack of cigarettes out of my shirt pocket and as I was lighting the weed, I suddenly realized how dumb what I was about to do really was. It was as if a light went on in my cortex warning me that sucking those noxious fumes down into my lungs defied some primal survival instinct. It actually scared me. A teen-aged Cuban lad was squatted on the beach nearby watching me, hoping that I would be kind enough to offer him a weed … or at least leave a long enough butt for him to enjoy. I tossed him the half-empty pack. He was profusely grateful, and now that I think about it I actually feel guilty for adding to his potential for an early demise. This happened as I said, in March 1985. What I didn't realize until several months later, was that it was exactly ten years earlier to the day that I had started to smoke again. And to make it even spookier, I had started to smoke while sitting on that **same beach**, in front of that **same hotel**, under that **same TREE** ten years earlier in Cuba !

Let's go back a bit. I started smoking at the age of fourteen. My cousin Billy was always ready to lead his younger cousin astray, and taught me how to do all of the things parents tell their kids not to do. He had a package of Tartan Cigarettes, a brand that was around for only a short time in Canada during the war. Like everything addictive, the first drag was quite a rush, and I spent a lot of time and money over the years trying to re-create that same rush. It never happened. About ten years later I was in the Canadian Air Force, and was transferred to a Canadian NATO Headquarters unit in France. In my usual perceptive way, I decided to quit smoking on the day of my transfer. It was perceptive, because in Europe, we had PXs where we could buy Canadian and American cigarettes for ten cents a pack ! A great time to quit smoking. However it was probably a wise decision, because at ten cents a pack, I could have smoked myself into a stupor. About ten years later I took a voluntarily release from the RCAF to pursue other interests. One of these interests was a sudden fascination with cigars and a pipe. More about that later. I was probably never meant to smoke in the first place, because every few years I'd quit cold turkey. It was at this point that we took our first of three vacation trips to Cuba. It was March 1975. I hadn't smoked for several years, and this was a totally terrific holiday for us. We had never been to a tropical island, a Communist country, or a resort hotel before. It was a time and place to experience everything. On the first day we met a group of lively and boisterous Canadians gathered around the patio in front of the Hotel Internacional. Cuba Libras (what else) were flowing like beer at a bar-b-q, and everybody was having a great time. One of the revelers had visited the local Cuban cigar outlet and picked up a box of Panatelas. Well after a few Cuba Libras, how can you not have a Cuban cigar? The impact of that cigar after several years of nicotine abstinence was very powerful. I had one of those out-of-body experiences that was both frightening and groovy at the same time. That was followed by an overwhelming desire to throw up, which I prevented by heading to my room and passing out for about two hours. When I woke up, I was totally hooked on those little cigars, and smoked dozens of them before we left the island. That was followed by ten years of very strong King-Size cigarettes. It was exactly ten years later that I had the rendezvous on the same beach with the Cuban kid. So you can see that I have quit many times … but this time it's forever ! All it takes is one drag on a weed to fall right back into the trap. It's happened to me, and it can happen to anyone who thinks that because they've been weed-free for a few months or even a few years, one cigarette won't hurt. Wrong! There's an insidious monster lurking inside every one of those slim paper tubes stuffed with that addictive weed… tobacco. It takes over your brain, your senses, your lungs and your wallet. The first puff after a long abstinence gives you a mini-rush which reminds you of the very first drag you took so long ago. It's a siren call to the slippery slopes of addiction, and believe me, it grabs you instantly and seductively. Why not have another…and another… and another ? Before you know it, you're trying to figure out how this happened, and how you can muster up the courage to quit ***… yet again !*** How about putting it into economic terms? Your own wallet for example. Just for the sake of keeping it simple, calculate the cost of smoking a pack a day at the cost of $6 a package. Multiply that by 365 and in one year you would have spent $2,190.00 Now multiply that by say fifty years. (If you start at age fifteen, chances are you MIGHT live another fifty years to age 65). That adds up to $109,500.00 And if your significant other is hooked, that adds up to $219,000.00 !!! Now if you take it one step further and calculate how much money you would have if you invested that $4,380.00 (for two smokers) every year in a safe investment portfolio, with compound interest you would have well over two million dollars at the age of 65.

Chapter 2

Here are two words that might make you think twice about your smoking addiction. **ERECTILE DYSFUNCTION**. Male smokers who puff a pack-a-day are risking a 60% chance of pricking the balloon of their sex lives. A recent very large study into the effects of smoking has concluded that even light smokers face a dysfunctional sexual future. The reason is this. Most young smokers don't worry about things like heart disease or lung cancer, but tell them that they won't be able to get an erection, and you might get their attention. Smoking causes atherosclerosis which is a build up of plaque inside the blood vessels. One of the body's largest concentrations of blood vessels is in the penis which is even more sensitive than the heart. But because of the differences in size, the penis' blood vessels are finer and clog easier. This slows the blood supply to this organ, and it's the blood that creates the erection. ***So light up and get limp!*** By the way, smoking also damages the male sperm, so if you want healthy, robust kids, quit the habit. The best advice obviously is to keep away from situations that invite the temptation to light up. However there are several aids to navigation to steer you away from the lure of the 'mini-fix'. We'll deal with those nav-aids in subsequent chapters, but first, let me tell you a little story. The first time I quit smoking, I was in my early twenties. I had smoked for several years, and was beginning to wonder why the hell I was wrecking my lungs for no apparent reason. At that time I was working for a Ford dealership in Detroit, across the river from my home in Windsor Ontario. It was a short commute, and besides my famous cousin Billy was living not far from the dealership with his parents, brothers and sisters. I spent many hours at their place after work, and got to know several of their friends. One of the lads who was pursuing my very pretty cousin 'Mickey' (Rosemary), was a very unusual guy named Lee. He was a jack-of-all-trades, one of which was (believe it or not) a pre-med assistant undertaker in a funeral home, where he performed pre-autopsy operations on the 'clients' in the back room. He invited my cousin Billy and me to watch as he performed one of his gruesome tasks, and it was my first inspiration to kick the habit. First of all, when we arrived in the chilly 'operating' room, I was a bit nervous, and perched on the edge of a table. It wasn't actually a table, it was a slab with a corpse stretched out on it. I accidentally sat on his leg. My instinctive "excuse me" generated a lot of laughs from my cousin and Lee. The operation began and included the removal of the brain, which I won't get into at this time. The important bit came when he opened up the cadaver's chest and removed a few (once) vital organs. When he came to the lungs, he said "Here's why you'll rarely find a pathologist or mortician who smokes." He pulled out a handful of what looked like black sea-weed. Coincidentally the 'patient' on the next table whose leg I had sat on had been the victim of a car accident. Lee reached in and showed us what a pair of healthy lungs looks like. The comparison was stunning. He said "Here's what thirty years of smoking does to your lungs … and here's what the lungs of a non-smoker look like." I immediately tossed my Pall Mall cigarettes into the garbage can, and that was it for me for a couple of years.

Why Not Smoke ?

The reasons why you shouldn't smoke would fill a book … but not this one. I'll just give you a few to think about, and you've probably read or heard about many of them, so I'll keep it brief. First of all, the famous lung-cancer incentive. Yeah, I know. You're going to tell me about your great-uncle or grand-pop who smoked two-packs a day and lived to be 103. Well good for them. There are actually people who jay-walk regularly and never get hit by a car. But there are also those who try it once and a big truck flattens them instantly. It's all about averages. Some folks manage to live forever, even though they totally abuse their systems and their bodies. Others try something once and it's game over. So pick a spot somewhere in between and if you make it that far, you've done OK. But why run the risk of snuffing it prematurely on the off-chance that you might accidentally survive in spite of sucking the smoke of 20 cigarettes a day into your lungs ? And it's not only your lungs you have to consider. Smoking actually causes ***bladder cancer !*** Lord knows why, but the noxious weed adversely affects nearly all of our vital and semi-vital organs. And the biggest organ of all …. (No, guys, that's not it!) … is ***the skin !*** So ladies, if you want to discover the fountain of youth, the elixir of 'youngness', the secret of eternal beauty,

QUIT SMOKING … NOW !

Years ago researchers conducted studies on mature sets of twins. Amazingly, they were able to find twin siblings where one was a smoker and the other a non-smoker. The studies showed that at the age of fifty, the average non-smoking twin had the skin characteristics of a forty-year-old. Conversely, the other twin with the 'habit' had the skin characteristics of a sixty-year-old ! Smoking prematurely ages your skin. Being the body's largest organ, the skin undergoes a massive assault on its life-giving attributes every time you light up a weed. (See chapter 4.) The lungs are an obvious target for the anti-smoking evangelists. I'm not in the category of an evangelist, by the way. If you want to smoke, go ahead. Just think about the consequences. The lungs function to exchange used carbon dioxide from our systems with fresh oxygen every time we take a breath. The methodology includes the action of millions of ***cilia***, tiny 'hairs' which line and cleanse the airways, and which wave back and forth continuously, enabling the oxygen to replace the carbon dioxide. At the first puff of a cigarette, the cilia go into a paralyzed state of shock, and the exchange is virtually shut down by a significant percentage. That's where the 'rush' occurs. Oxygen deprivation and other factors make us dizzy and semi-euphoric, which the drug translates into "feelin' good". It takes the cilia several hours to get back to their normal function, but in the meantime a certain amount of damage has occurred… and that damage builds up with each cigarette. If it doesn't develop into cancer, it will very possibly turn into emphysema. In fact, cigarette smoking is the main cause of chronic bronchitis and COPD ~ Chronic Obstructive Pulmonary Disease. Smoking marijuana is even more toxic. All of the medical text books strongly recommend that the single most important step folks who suffer from bronchitis, asthma or emphysema should take, is to quit smoking .... period. "Any smoker with a persistent cough needs regular check-ups to screen for lung cancer and other tobacco-related diseases" accoding to leading medical journals. The average healthy adult inhales and exhales an average of ten to fifteen times a minute. This is accomplished without any conscious effort, and provides every body cell with essential oxygen. Smoking seriously interferes with this natural process. The nicotine creates the addiction but it's the sixty other chemicals that cause the cancer. However nicotine may possibly be a more dangerous culprit than previously thought. The cellular genetic damage caused by those 60 chemicals causes old damaged cells that are programmed to 'commit suicide' when their useful life is over, to stick around. These cells degenerate to the point where they can become cancerous. It's the nicotine that sets up an enzyme reaction that interferes with cellular suicide. Within minutes the nicotine activates the enzyme called AKT which blocks cell suicide and makes them more vulnerable to carcinogen agents. Scientists have known about this phenomenon for many years, but the actual enzyme was not pin-pointed until recently. Knowing the structure of the enzyme could lead to more effective cancer-preventing drugs.

Quit recently ?

Chapter 3

This is the chapter that will convince you to quit the weed !!

(I hope)

Over the years I've discussed the significance of quitting the weed with many friends and colleagues. I haven't been 'preachy' about it. Nobody wants to listen to a reformed smoker with a message. But I have acknowledged the difficulties facing a smoker who desperately wants to quit. There's a short tale and small illustration I occasionally offer any smoker who shows a genuine desire to knock it off, and it goes like this :

Every drag on a cigarette is sucked down the wind-pipe **(a)** where it impacts on the bronchial divide **(b)** which is located just below and behind the notch in your neck. This area is about the same size as your finger knuckle when you bend your fore-finger… an area about the size of a dime. The smoke and tar and carcinogens and impurities divide at this point and head off into your left and right lungs, where they do a number on your afore-mentioned cilia. Meanwhile, back at the bronchial divide, something sinister is happening. If you calculate how many cells there are in the little dot **(c)**, you will count about a million cells. It'll take awhile, but trust me … there are a million. If you extrapolate that and expand it into the area about the size of a dime on your bronchial divide, forget about the numbers. Too many to count. However each one of these zillions of cells is very important, because each one is a potential cancer cell. If you remember your experience as a person who has locked him/herself out of the car, you may recall having to do some fancy acrobatics with a coat hanger. By bending the hanger repeatedly at the same spot, it eventually develops metal fatigue and breaks off at that point. What happens with each of those bazillions of cells on your bronchial divide is very similar. Every one of those cells becomes stressed out, and instead of happily going through its several-year life-span looking roughly like **(d)**, it goes into spasm and looks something like **(e)**. This is not good. This is a pre-cancerous mode. And there are a lot of them in there. It just takes one more drag on a weed… maybe the NEXT one … to have just one of those countless little cells ***(over which you have absolutely no control)*** to flip over into ---

(f) -mode - a cancer cell… which quickly divides in two. All you need is one of these little suckers, and within hours, you have **(g)** twice as many. Shortly after, you have **(h)** … twice as many again … and then **(i)** … you've got it … ***twice as many again !*** And the doubling game goes on and on and on … until voila … it's too late. There's a nice big cancer tumor in your throat. And by that time it's probably metastasized to your liver, stomach, lungs, prostate, pancreas … and brain. Isn't smoking fun ? The good news is that there's a pretty good chance that your little cell **(e)** is still only in a state of shock, and if you're convinced that quitting is a good idea, you might arrest the negative direction this little sucker is heading in. Actually folks who quit while they're ahead are rewarded with the knowledge that these renegade cells usually repair themselves and begin to look like normal cells within a couple of years. So that's my brief sermon on just one of the many reasons why it's a good idea to think about kicking the habit … and I don't mean booting a nun in the butt. I'm pleased to claim that I have successfully convinced a significant number of people in one-on-one conversations to quit smoking ***permanently*** with this little story. (See diagram on next page).

Here's why you should quit smoking.

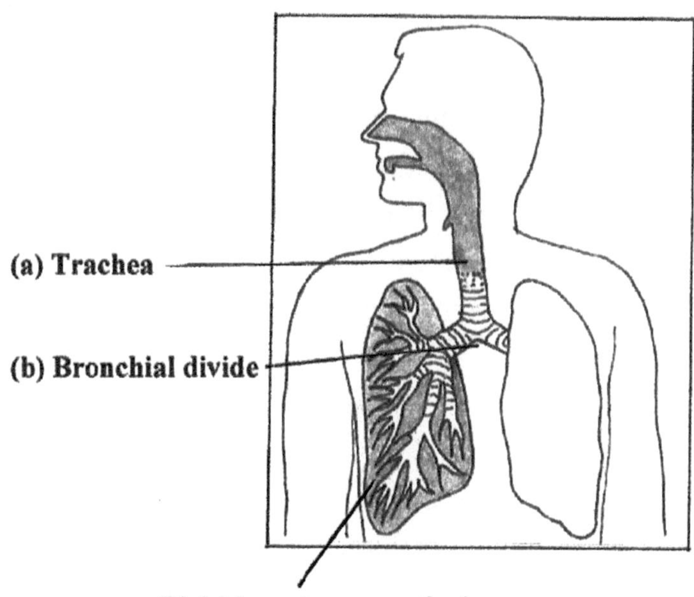

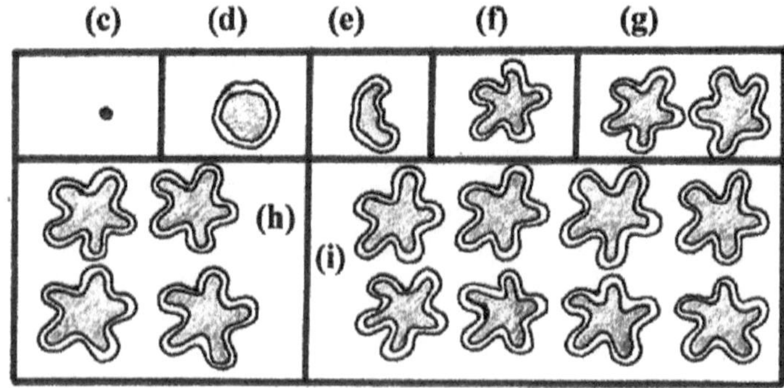

Chapter 4

Meanwhile, back to the premature aging of the skin. A recent story out of London bore the head-line: **"Smoking robs skin's elasticity: Scientists".** The sub-head said: ***"Researchers now know why smokers age prematurely"*** and the story went on to say: "Smokers look older than non-smokers because tobacco triggers a protein that attacks the skin's elasticity. The protein breaks down collagen, the fibrous material that helps to prevent wrinkles, according to scientists from the Guy's, King's and Thomas' School of Medicine in London. The change is thought to be irreversible and cannot be restored with dietary supplements. Smokers who sun-bathe wrinkle faster because the sun's ultra-violet rays also encourage anti-collagen protein in the skin. Smoking has long been associated with premature aging. A study in the American Journal of Public Health in 1995 said the faces of 20-a-day smokers aged by 14 years for every ten years of smoking. But the reason has not been clearly understood. The protein, known as Matrix Metallo-proteinase-1 (MMP-1) was found by accident during a study of ultra-violet light and aging on 33 volunteers. Researchers were at a loss to explain why background levels of MMP-1 were much higher on some volunteers, until they asked about their smoking habits. Anthony Young, a professor based at the medical school, said: "It was a highly significant result and very unlikely to be due to chance. Smoking exerts such a noticeable effect on the skin that it is often possible to detect whether or not a person is a smoker simply by looking at his or her face. Smokers have more wrinkles and their skin tends to have a grayish pallor."

Well, what do you think of that ? All of those expensive night creams, skin lotions, exotic oils, wrinkle removers, enriched moisturizers, pick-up creams and other assorted miracle potions are not going to help if you smoke. Just look in the mirror and ask yourself "Do I look like a smoker ?" If the answer is "Yes" … it's time to think about quitting.

Too Old to Quit?

Your quality of life will radically improve when you quit smoking. And a recent study by Duke University has concluded that you will also live longer… no matter how old you are when you quit. Even 65-year-old smokers who quit lasted longer than their friends of the same age who kept on smoking. Many other studies have proven that you can drastically lower your risk of heart disease, cancer and respiratory problems. But only recently have studies shown that reformed smokers definitely live longer than their peers who continue puffing on the weed. And this was not a small local survey. The tests took over 15 years, and the sample included smokers and quitters from all parts of the U.S. Data showed that people could add more years to their lives if they quit earlier. Men who stopped smoking at 35 years of age lived approximately 8 years longer than men who kept smoking. The expectancy rate is lower in older quitters, however even at 65 years of age, they lived from one to two years longer. And women were even better off. They added three to four years to their lives if they quit at age 65.

You can make it easier to quit. Join a health club or start exercising at home. It can make you feel good about yourself and your decision to quit. However there will be moments when the urge is more overwhelming, and that's when your will-power and self- control have to kick in. Here are a few tips that might help avoid or overcome those moments of temptation:

- Try to avoid alcohol, coffee and other beverages you associate with smoking.
- Keep your hands occupied by playing with a paper clip, pencil or a coin.
- Try to avoid people, places or situations that you identified with smoking.
- It's most difficult after a meal, so try brushing your teeth, or going for a walk instead. A glass of water can work wonders!
- Each month on the anniversary of the day you quit, reward yourself with a special treat. And finally, if you

do relapse, don't panic. Most people who successfully quit the habit have only done so after several attempts.

Here are some facts and figures from the Cancer Society. Your body begins a series of physiological changes almost as soon as you throw away your last cigarette.

- **Within 20 minutes:** Blood pressure, body temperature and pulse rate will drop to nearly normal.
- **Within eight hours:** Smoker's breath disappears. The carbon monoxide level in blood drops, and the oxygen level rises to normal.
- **Within 24 hours**: Chance of heart attack decreases.
- **Within 48 hours:** Nerve endings start to regroup. Ability to taste and smell improves.
- **Within three days:** Breathing is easier.
- **Within 2 - 3 months:** Circulation improves. Walking becomes easier. Lung capacity increases up to 30%
- **Within 1 - 9 months:** Sinus congestion and shortness of breath decrease. Cilia that sweep debris from your lungs begin to grow back. Energy increases.
- **Within one year:** Excess risk of coronary heart disease is half that of a person who smokes.
- **Within two years:** Heart attack risk drops to near normal.
- **Within five years:** Lung cancer rate for an average former pack-a-day smoker decreases by almost half. Stroke risk is reduced. Risk of mouth, throat and esophageal cancer is half that of a smoker.

- **Within 10 years:** Lung cancer death rate is similar to that of a person who does not smoke. The pre-cancerous cells are replaced.
- **Within 15 years:** Risk of coronary heart disease is the same as a person who has never smoked.

U.S. Health care costs have risen to $65 billion a year because of smoking.

Atherosclerosis, various types of cancer, cardiovascular disease, and clogged arteries are the chief contributors to the cause of death from smoking.

Fred! We've been looking for you since last Tuesday !

Chapter 5

The unique pleasure derived from smoking a cigarette is occasionally ruined by unforeseen events. A very good friend of mine has been a non-smoker for many years, but he still recalls a couple of incidents involving smoking that make him wonder what makes people do it. He was with his future wife in a movie theater one evening. (She specifically told me NOT to use their real names.) Somehow they managed to sit in one of the rows of seats where smoking was prohibited. In those days every other row was a smoking area! Go figure ! Anyhow, the usher showed up and asked him to put out his cigarette or move. He decided to 'nip' the lit end off the cigarette and put the butt in his shirt pocket. No, his shirt didn't catch fire. But when he pinched the smoldering end off the weed, it fell into his pant-cuff. A few moments later dozens of panicky people were looking for the source of the smoke. It took him a few seconds to realize that his pants were on fire.

In that same theater a couple of years later, the same pal and the same girl who was by now his wife, were enjoying a movie. Earlier that day, my friend, who was a Leading Aircraftsman in the RCAF (nearly the lowest rank in the Air Force) … had convinced one of his pals to lend him his brand new Air Force 'officer-style' uniform cap. He wanted to impress his parents and his new bride with this very upscale head-gear. Now this was a very special cap. At that time the junior ranks were issued 'wedge' caps which were worn by non-commissioned air-men. Only the officers had peaked 'flat-tops'. That month a special group of airmen had been issued the new peaked junior-ranks 'flat-tops'. They were the special Honor-Guard, and they were the only ones allowed to wear these snazzy caps. So when my friend was able to convince his pal to lend him his hat, it was really something special. He promised to guard it with his life. So there they sat in the darkened theater. My pal proudly in his uniform, and his new wife proudly sitting beside him, holding the precious hat in her lap … and a cigarette in her hand. Once again the theater patrons were distracted by their search for the source of the clouds of smoke. Once again it was my friend's attire … or rather ***his pal's*** attire that was smoldering. His bride was so engrossed in the movie that she didn't notice that she was resting the hot end of the cigarette on the top of the very special hat. It would have been hard to explain a large burn hole in the top of a brand-new very special flat-top hat to the owner of said hat. It would have been impossible to buy a replacement. So my friend cleverly solved the problem. He took the belt from one of his blue uniforms which matched the material in the hat, brought it to an invisible mending establishment, and the hat looked as good as new. He doesn't smoke any more. His wife does, but not around hats. By the way, my friend went on to earn an officer's flat-top with gold braid attached. He retired as a Squadron Leader (Major) with great honor.

Here's something to think about. What would you suggest as a penalty for those bozos who decide it's time to empty their over-flowing ashtrays in the parking lots of shopping centers? My choice would be to make them eat their own cigarette-butt sandwiches.

Chapter 6

One of the mysteries about the craving for a cigarette is that it often really isn't a weed that the addict is craving ! Research shows that our sub-conscious cortex regularly receives specific messages that we need something. A smoker usually assumes that this is a signal to light up a cigarette. That primal signal is actually saying ***'I'M THIRSTY !'*** Nine times out of ten the 'thirst' signal is misconstrued by the smoker to mean 'time for a weed'. So they light up. The thirst often goes unquenched, and the mild dehydration experienced by most smokers continues. That's why one of the most important weapons in the 'quit smoking' arsenal is a bottle of water in your pocket. If you're carrying bottled water in your pocket or purse, or keep it on your desk or in your car or in your brief-case at all times, and if you respond to that 'nicotine fit' syndrome with a good belt of H20 instead, you're more than half way there. That, coupled with a few of packs of gum or some small hard candies, and you'll beat the fidgets big time. Of course there are times when the urge is nearly totally over-powering. Have you ever noticed the actions of smokers in a casino? When a smoker hits any kind of jack-pot on the slots … even a medium/ smallish one … they will automatically and instantaneously light up a weed. It happens absolutely 100% of the time. Have you ever noticed the actions of a smoker under any kind of pressure ? They will automatically reach for a cigarette. Give a smoker a cup of coffee and out come the butts. Enjoy a great meal in a fine restaurant, and when it's time for the liquors, it's time for a smoke. And there's the famous cigarette ***"afterwards."*** There are triggers to the habit. The key is to identify these behavior catalysts, and do something to short-circuit them. Completely avoiding these trigger situations is neither possible nor practical. A smoker would have to become a hermit. One recommended solution is to know what situations stimulate these actions, and be prepared for them. That way a smoker who really wants to kick the habit can arm him/ herself with the psychological weapons they'll need. Birthdays are often memorable and occasionally out-standing events. Most of the many ***many*** birthdays I've experienced fortunately fall into the first category. There are a few, however which fit the 'outstanding' classification. One was when my wife and I were given a wonderful cruise vacation by a group of friends for one of my milestone annual rituals which happened recently. Then there was my memorable 25th birthday which took place on the beautiful island of Mallorca. And of course the big family get-togethers to mark other birth-dates that ended in zero. But It was several years ago when my late wife Terry gave me the best birthday present I've ever received. She quit smoking …***and she stuck with it*** **!**

She had quit twice in the past, once for nearly a year. But the temptation always got the better of her. This time she really stretched her will power to the max, and I'm proud to say that she found it uncomfortable to be in a room where there are smokers.

❧ ☙

And by the way, smoking pot is several times more dangerous to your respiratory system than ordinary cigarettes. Hash and 'Mary-Jane' users seem to think that because what they're smoking doesn't contain tobacco it won't harm their lungs. WRONG! In fact because pot-smokers tend to drag hard, inhale deep and hold it in as long as possible, the damage to their breathing apparatus is multiplied significantly. However, there can be interesting spin-offs to the fight against growing illegal substances.

Here's one. The phone rings at Mountie headquarters. "RCMP Detachment, Constable Rogers speaking." Voice: "Hello, I don't want to be a fink, but I'm fed up with Travis Jones down the road. He's hiding marijuana in his firewood pile." "Thank you very much for your call sir." The next day the RCMP agents descend on Jones' house. They search the shed where the firewood is kept. Using axes, they chop open every piece of firewood, but find no marijuana. They threaten Jones, but have to leave due to lack of evidence. Later the phone rings at Jones' house. "Hey Travis ! Did the Mounties come to your house ?" "Yeah." "Did they chop your firewood?" "Yep."

"Great. Now it's your turn to call. I need my garden plowed."

A recent study from the University of Sydney Nova Scotia has found that employees who take outside smoke-breaks take longer, harder and more frequent puffs on cigarettes than smokers in social settings. A Director of the Stop Smoking Program, said the practice results in smokers dying earlier because they take in higher doses of carcinogens and contaminants.

Which bundle did I put my cigarettes in ?

Chapter 7

With three adult daughters, I'm very happy to report that only one of them smokes. And when they were growing up in the seventies and eighties, it's a miracle they didn't all become addicted to cigarettes ... or worse ! As they were growing up I was quite concerned about the peer pressure they would face when they became teen-agers and entered high school. Kids that age are vulnerable to the opinions and examples they encounter, particularly in grades 8, 9 and 10. If an older or more aggressive student approached them with an offer to share a cigarette or a joint, what's a kid supposed to do or say ? If they beg off by saying "My parents would object" or "I'm afraid to try that", they would be teased or mocked into giving in. This pressure becomes especially difficult to resist when there's a house party or school dance. The young 'victim' feels as if they're in a spot-light when someone offers them a cigarette or perhaps some 'designer' drug. They can't find a non-wimpy way to say no, and they desperately want to fit in and be part of the 'cool' school crowd... so they often give-in out of embarrassment. After pondering this dilemma for some time, I came up with a very simple, yet effective defense against the insidious peer pressure that so often plagues youngsters in these situations. I sat down with my daughters and explained that these situations were going to come up, and that if they were going to be uncomfortable trying to figure out how to say **NO**, I offered them a suggestion. Their faces lit up immediately, and they couldn't wait to try my idea. It was simple. Here's what I suggested to them.

"When someone offers you anything you don't want to accept ... a cigarette, a drink, maybe even some kind of drug, it will be difficult to say no because you feel that everybody is watching you. Maybe you're embarrassed to say that your parents would be upset. All you have to tell the person offering something to you, is this:

'I tried that once and I threw up all over everything.'

Nobody wants to see anyone throw up all over everything, so they back-off and stop pressuring you to do something that isn't right. Years later I was very pleased to hear that this strategy actually worked more than once for my kids. I've passed this little 'escape plan' along to my grandchildren. Maybe it'll work for a youngster you know.

Then of course we have well-meaning celebrities who are doing their best to further the cause of non-smoking, but somehow manage to screw it up. For example, a very beautiful and well-intentioned movie star was allegedly being interviewed to become an anti-smoking spokesperson for a national non-smoking campaign. She earnestly spoke to the camera, saying "Smoking kills …. And if you're killed, you lose a very important part of your life."

❧ ❧

I recently wrote a rather politically incorrect book entitled "Women Can't Merge, Men Won't Yield". It's based on the 'Venus/Mars' principle as it applies to driving. In it, I devoted a few words to smoking while driving, and at the risk of offending anyone who might actually have read the other book, I thought it might be a good idea to include those thoughts in this book.

'Never smoke a pipe while driving. When I used to smoke, occasionally I'd dig out my old pipe and puff on it for a couple of weeks until I couldn't stand it any-more. Several times while shoulder checking to my left with the pipe between my teeth, I've driven the pipe-stem down my throat as it slammed into the window. This is usually accompanied by a shower of burning embers from the pipe bowl. These embers always land in your lap, and as you calmly extract the pipe from your gullet and try to nonchalantly put out the flames in your crotch area with a cup of coffee, (which turns out to be very hot), you notice that you are at a stop light beside a large city bus. The amused bus passengers seem to enjoy your frantic antics with the burning pants, however many of them don't realize that you've actually ignited your trousers and give you nasty looks. They naturally assume that you're some kind of exhibitionist pervert. The situation is always made more interesting when you notice that one of the passengers glaring at you is the lady from your office building you've been admiring from afar for 3 years.

The flaming-lap scenario happens more frequently with cigarette smokers. Occasionally a cigarette held between the lips for a certain period of time will sort of 'weld' itself to the lower lip. The smoker doesn't know that the cigarette is stuck there much like the way your tongue sticks to a frozen iron post. When he/she nonchalantly grasps the middle of the weed between the index and middle finger a la Humphry Bogart, and attempts to remove it from between the lips, the cigarette actually stays stuck to the lip. The fingers slide very quickly along the paper tube and *past* the lit end. A frenzied flurry of activity takes place when the entire burning end of the weed comes off between the fingers. Part of the glowing ember attaches itself ***to*** the fingers. The rest of the red-hot material flies all over the inside of the car in a flurry of sparks. It's enough to make some folks actually think about giving up the weed.

Setting the back seat on fire is more common than most smokers realize. It happens when the smokaholic driver finishes the latest cigarette and tries to poke it out of the driver's side window, which has been opened about one inch. The smoker sees the butt fly out the window in a shower of sparks … but what they often miss is the re-entry of the butt further back along the same window. It always lands in the rear seat area, and unless the driver notices the problem, it can smolder for a long time before bursting into flames. This can be very annoying for back-seat passengers. A variation of this situation happens when the smoking driver flicks the butt out of the window and then realizes that the window was closed. With any luck the red-hot weed won't ricochet off the glass and down the front of his shirt.'

Those excerpts were from my previous book about driving. My apologies.

A heavy smoker was trying to quit, and during his two-week follow-up appointment with his cardiologist, he informed the doctor that he was having trouble with the prescribed medication. "Which one?" the doctor asked. "The patch. The nurse told me to put on a new one every six hours, and now I'm running out of places to stick them." When the doctor examined him, he was covered with patches.

Nearly all reformed smokers are able to provide the exact date, and often the exact time they renounced the weed. It's a genuine life-altering decision … a fork in the road of your time on this planet. Recently a young, vital healthy lady told me her story. She had smoked for many years, and with the approach of an entirely brand new millennium, she vowed that she would never smoke in the 21st century. At exactly midnight, when the 20th century ticked over to the year 2000, she tossed her remaining cigarettes into the waste basket. About three months later she was experiencing a combination of second thoughts, personal crises, fifteen pounds of unexpected additional avoirdupois, and an overwhelming craving for a weed. It was her weekly day to meet her mother at the shopping center, and as she left her home she drove towards the nearest corner store to buy a pack of cigarettes. She inadvertently drove right past the store. "Oh well" she thought. "I'll just stop at the next 711 down the street." The next thing she knew she was at the shopping center, and still no weeds. She met her mother in the parking lot, and said "I'm just going into the grocery store for a minute." The craving was gnawing at her nerve-ends. As she headed across the parking lot towards the store, she suddenly felt a wave of guilt wash over her. "What am I doing ? I've just gone through three months of self-discipline and withdrawal, and now I'm going to give up and have a cigarette? Maybe three or four ?" A moment of hesitation and she thought "Damn right I am." But looking skyward in a flash of desperation, she pleaded "Please, God … give me a sign and I won't do this." Exactly two seconds later, an ambulance raced by with sirens blaring. She stared resentfully at the retreating vehicle, looked up and said "Not good enough!" She marched into the store and headed for the smokes counter. Suddenly a friend she hadn't seen for many months approached her. My friend was astonished, because this person had quit smoking some time ago, and her sudden appearance had seemed like an omen. "You are my sign!" she exclaimed. The startled woman had no idea what was happening, but my friend looked skyward again and said "Thank you, Thank you." Her friend still doesn't know what that was all about, but that chance meeting did the trick. My friend still has not smoked in the 21st century.

I asked another good friend if she had any interesting 'quit smoking' stories. She is a type AA, very active, quite funny and refreshingly outspoken. Here's her very short response.

"I gave up smoking and decided to jog. I threw the smokes out and took off at a canter, went two blocks, fell in my friend's front door and demanded a cigarette or I would kill her on the spot. Thank God she had one. It's the one and only time I ever tried to quit, and thank God it didn't last long."

Which anti-smoking scare story is stuck to the fridge today ?

Chapter 8

When I was a teen-ager, I had a summer job in a plate-glass factory. I was a 'glass-finisher' which meant I worked at a sanding belt which revolved at amazing speed. The object was to grind the very sharp edges off pieces of glass. These strips of glass which measured from 2 X 6 inches to 5 X 24 inches were called "Woolworth Glass", because they were used to separate the variety of items displayed on the sales counters in the Woolworth stores. I was a diligent worker, but I still have the scars on my knuckles from the edge of that infernal sand-paper belt that whizzed past my fingers at about 10,000 miles an hour. One of the things I did to pass the time during the infrequent breaks or when the machinery stopped running, was to head into the warehouse and do about a hundred push-ups and a hundred 'chin-ups'. I was a wiry but muscular lad, and at that time I had stopped smoking for awhile because I was on a fitness rampage. Everyone else in the building smoked like fiends. There were burning cigarette butts every-where, and the edges of every table and countertop bore the dark brown and black burns of forgotten smokes. It was actually amazing to watch a glass cutting expert carefully etch the cutting lines on a huge plate of glass, while wisps of smoke from the cigarette between his teeth curled straight up into his eyes. Tears streaming down his cheeks from his burning eyes, and a hacking cough didn't cause him to waver one bit. But it eventually killed him. He was my uncle. I was also the staff cartoonist, and the janitor was a particularly avid smoker, so I did this little cartoon of him, along with the following poem:

Tobacco is a rotten weed - I like it.
It satisfies no human need - I like it.
It makes you thin, it makes you lean,
It takes the hair right off your bean,
It's the worst damn stuff I've ever seen...I like it.

I think that sums up the love/hate feeling that most smokers have about their habit.

Remembering the exact time, date and circumstances of quitting smoking is like everyone over a certain age can recall exactly where they were on November 23rd, 1963, when they heard the words "The President has been shot". I've asked a few pals if they had any recollections about their quitting experience, and here are a few. Bert is a television news cameraman. He was in the National Press Club of Canada one evening after returning from a NATO junket to Europe. He had run out of Canadian cigarettes in Belgium, so he bought a pack of very strong Belgian smokes. They were virtually killing him, and when he reached for one at the club bar, he said "enough is enough" and tossed them in the waste bin. He hasn't smoked since, and he remembers exactly when that happened. 7 p.m. June 30th, 1965.

- A good friend of mine who happens to be a very successful businessman and excellent role model, told me about his exper-ience with kicking the habit. I'll call him Tom. Quite a few years ago when his son was in his early teens, the lad approached his father about the startling and rather frightening things he had been learning is school about the perils of smoking. Obviously the message is getting through to some of the kids. He was worried about his father's health, and asked him if he might consider quitting smoking. Tom saw an excellent opportunity to accomplish two things at once. He had always wanted to have a good excuse to give up cigarettes, and he was anxious to give his son some motivation to improve his grades in school. "I'll make a deal with you," Tom said. "If you can show me three report cards in a row with some improvement in your marks, I'll quit smoking."

His son was delighted with the challenge, and sure enough his next three report cards showed significant improvement. Tom lived up to his end of the deal … almost. One evening after an excellent dinner with guests, Tom couldn't resist the temptation to light up 'just one cigarette'. He bummed a weed from one of their guests, sneaked down to the nearest bathroom and lit up. What a rush. And what a moment of panic! He was just starting to enjoy himself when he heard footsteps running down the hall towards the bathroom, and the voice of his son calling to him. "Dad, dad, guess what!" Tom threw the butt into the toilet bowl, flushed it down and frantically waved a towel around to disperse the smoke. The door burst open and his excited son said, "Hey dad I ……". He paused, sniffed the air and said "Have you been smoking dad?" Tom sheepishly said "I was just having one cigarette son. It was a big mistake. Sorry about that. Now what was it you wanted to tell me?" His son slowly walked away and said "It wasn't important dad." At that moment Tom felt as if he had totally betrayed his son's confidence and faith in him. He was devastated. And he never smoked again!

-Another media colleague of mine (media types seem to be heavy smokers … among other things) was on his way to Hawaii recently for a holiday. While he was there with his lady-love, they decided to get married. I like spontaneity. However Bob is a very staunch smoker, and the thought of a direct nonstop 12-hour flight from Toronto to Hawaii without the comfort of a nicotine fix was too much. He opted for a nicotine patch, which he purchased at a drug store in Toronto the day before the flight. Unfortunately Bob was a bit distracted by the complexities of getting it all together for the trip, and he left the patch in the hotel room. Although his fingernails were totally nibbled to the quick by the time they landed in Hawaii, he managed to survive. However he made a point of finding a drug store and asking for another patch. He wasn't going through that again. The pharmacist led Bob to the back of the shop, unlocked a special cabinet and took out a slim package containing one patch. "That'll be $35.00" smiled the druggist. "Are you nuts?" howled Bob. "I bought one of those things in Toronto for ten dollars Canadian. That's equal to six dollars U.S. ! What the hell is this thirty-five dollars?" It was no good arguing, and Bob, being a true frugal Canuck decided to let his nails grow for the rest of the vacation so he'd have something to do on the return flight. No way was he going to spend $35.00 U.S. ($50.00 Canadian) for a damned patch ! When he told me this tale, I immediately concocted a lucrative scheme to make a lot of money and enjoy a nice Hawaiian vacation. I'm not going to tell you what it is.

As we go through life we come across examples of incredible behavior that almost defy belief. Here's one you can see at any time of the day, outside any large hospital in any city in the world. You'll see a gurney outside the acute care ward, with a patient festooned with tubes, electronic bleeping machines, bags of antibiotics and solutions, looking like he/she's a hiccup away from the crematorium .... ***enjoying a nice cigarette !***

And in Canada, that scene can be spotted even in the dead of winter, at 20 below. Just add a tinge of blue and an uncontrollable shivering action to the patient. Come on folks, how desperate for a fix can you be?

The condemned man was chained to a post in the prison courtyard. The firing squad was lined up twenty feet away. They loaded their rifles. The squad captain strode up to the prisoner and pinned a target on his chest. He reached into his tunic pocket and took out a package of cigarettes. "Would you care for a final cigarette?" he asked. The prisoner looked at the soldier scornfully and said, "No thanks. I'm trying to quit."

I wish they'd fix that draft near my desk.

Chapter 9

Did you know that smoking can cause you to lose your teeth? The Canadian Dental Association has taken aim at smoking as a significant cause of tooth loss, and has produced an attention-grabbing poster headlined **"Don't let tobacco spoil your smile".** It goes on to say "You are probably aware that tobacco can cause heart disease and a variety of cancers. What you may not know is that tobacco is a major cause of tooth loss in adults. The truth is, it's a lot harder to look and feel your best if you use tobacco products. If you smoke, talk to your dentist today about how tobacco is affecting your oral health." The Association claims that stained teeth and unpleasant breath are not the most serious results of smoking. Smokers are far more likely to develop oral cancer, and are four times more likely to develop periodontal disease which often leads to tooth loss and other complications. If you're looking for support and information on quitting the weed, your dentist could be your first line of defense. Most smokers have heard all the tales about lung cancer and other smoking related diseases, but few are aware of the increasing numbers of oral cancer victims. It's a frightening prospect to look forward to the pain and disfiguring results of oral cancer in your senior years. That's one possible prognosis if you smoke most of your adult life. Statistics show that about 90% of dentists discuss smoking with their patients, and approximately 60% warned their patients of the probable oral risks they face down the road. Occasionally a frank conversation with their dentist is all the motivation it takes for a smoker to give up the habit. Sometimes a simple professional cleaning by a dental technician will provide the incentive. The smoker likes that clean feeling, and doesn't want to ruin it with tobacco. One indicator of gum disease triggered by tobacco is called Leukoplakia. That's the white patches on the gums, signaling a pre-cancerous change to the soft tissues of the mouth. Fortunately, quitting smoking can often cause these lesions to disappear very quickly. Such information coming from their dentist can be very convincing, since it's often unexpected. Dentists are concerned that smoking is killing thousands of people every year, and as health professionals they are anxious to help in the fight to get people to 'butt-out'. Of course, dentists are also alarmed at the rising fad of body-piercing among young people, particularly in and around the mouth. One of the worst offenders is the pierced tongue. This dangerous trend can lead to nerve damage, infections, broken teeth, and even potentially deadly illnesses such as hepatitis. When a tongue is pierced it opens up a direct route to the body for serious infections to invade the body. The mouth is an active breeding reservoir for bacteria, and the immune system is constantly fighting off the bacterial invasion. A piercing can very quickly become seriously infected and lead to septicemia and toxic shock syndrome, which can be fatal. Some of the 'jewelry' worn in the mouth has been accidentally swallowed and the wearer has aspirated or choked to death on the tiny bar- bells. But smoking is still the most serious long-term medical risk among younger folks. Between the ages of 20 and 24, 30% of women and 35% of men smoke. That's the highest smoking rate by category in the survey. Will a younger person quit smoking when they realize that they could lose their teeth as they get older? Ask them.

Out of Breath ? Wonder Why ?

Are you having a bit more trouble getting your breath after minor exertion? Do you feel as though you aren't getting as much oxygen in your lungs as you used to? Time to get a check up for Chronic Obstructive Pulmonary Disease … COPD. Breathlessness and fatigue are not necessarily part of the aging process … unless you're a smoker. And more than 90% of victims of this insidious disease are smokers. Fatigue is just one of the symptoms of COPD. A chronic cough usually accompanies the condition, and it is aggravated by winter colds and flu. COPD is usually a combination of emphysema and chronic bronchitis, resulting from years of cigarette smoking. Symptoms don't usually appear until the lung damage has become irreversible. COPD strikes 15 to 20 percent of smokers. It's the fifth most common cause of death, and the explanation for one in five hospitalizations. Symptoms usually begin to appear in smokers aged 65 or more, and with the approaching wave of boomers and gen Xers, the numbers will increase dramatically. Unfortunately the public isn't aware of the significance of these statistics, and concern over the seriousness of COPD is slow to catch on. But the drastic effects of smoking on the lungs are obvious to health care workers … and to pathologists. For example emphysema destroys the elasticity of the lungs so that they can't 'squeeze' the old air out after the lungs have been filled. This inability to force the used air out of the lungs means that it's difficult to take a deep breath. The inability to inhale fresh air causes that out-of-breath, or shortness of breath feeling, and it leads to chronic fatigue. When the airways that branch down into the lungs become inflamed, they create mucous to protect themselves from this irritation. The cilia, thousands of tiny hair-thin shapes that detect contaminants help to stimulate coughing to clear the airways, are trapped in this excessive mucous. This causes the airways to become clogged and results in shortness of breath. Bacteria thrive in this environment, and infections are common to people with chronic bronchitis. Because these symptoms are not obvious until it's too late, smokers should undergo regular examinations of their lung function. Early diagnosis and life-style management changes are the only preventive measure available. Number one on the list is a smoking cessation program. Quit the weed. If asthma is present, get treatment. Lungs stressed by COPD are vulnerable to flu and pneumonia. Get your annual flu shot. If you are experiencing breathing problems, get it diagnosed. Antibiotics can be helpful in preventing bacterial inflammations if caught early. If you want to avoid the onset of these conditions and the need to take 'breathing lessons', 'oxygen therapy', 'puffer techniques', and that 'puffed out' feeling, think twice before lighting up that next coffin-nail. Vasoconstriction is another pleasant side-effect of smoking. That fancy term describes a condition whereby the smaller arteries shut down. The muscles in their walls suddenly contract because of the nicotine. If you're a smoker and you suffer from chronic cold hands and feet, chances are that the nicotine is affecting circulation to your extremities. This leads to a cold sensation, numbness, pallor and tingling. Taking it one step further, nicotine can cause coronary artery spasm as well. That's the part of your body that supplies blood to your heart, and has led to many smoking related heart attacks and strokes. If you want your circulation to improve, quit the weed.

Tobacco companies spend $15,000 a minute to advertise their products.

Listen to This Doctor

Doctor Peter Gott is probably one of the most recognized syndicated medical columnists and diagnosticians in North America. His column is read by millions of readers every day, and often contains advice related to the perils of smoking. One of his recent responses to a reader pointed out the vital importance of quitting smoking, and the sooner the better. Dr. Gott has given me permission to reprint the following.

Smokers at Higher Risk of Cancer

DEAR DR. GOTT: My uncle, a two-pack-a-day smoker, quit cigarettes in his 40s. At 80, he was diagnosed with lung cancer and subsequently died. The doctors blamed it on cigarettes, but I thought that ex-smoker's lungs returned to normal after having been 'clean' for five to ten years. Couldn't he have developed cancer whether or not he smoked?

DEAR READER: Of course he could have. The cause of lung cancer remains a mystery. However it is not a mystery that cigarette smoking is strongly related to lung cancer. In fact, the burgeoning incidence of such cancers in today's middle-age women directly reflects the increased use of cigarettes in the female population. To a large degree the pulmonary consequences of tobacco smoke are permanent; they are a function of the intensity and duration of the smoking habit. Thus, a person who smokes two cigarettes a day for forty years is less likely to develop cancer than is the two-pack-a-day smoker who quits after 20 years. Once a person gives up tobacco, his or her lung efficiency may improve up to 20 or 30%. The risk of chronic pulmonary ailments such as bronchitis and emphysema, lessens. But that person is still at higher risk for cancer. Therefore it behooves all smokers to stop as soon as possible, even though such a positive decision may not fully protect against the ultimate problem of malignancy. In addition, I do not know what other carcinogens your uncle may have been exposed to. As you know, this is a topic of fairly recent concern among people who, in the 1940s and 50s were unknowingly placed in dangerous workplaces where asbestos, hydrocarbons, and other carcinogens were common. In summary, although much pulmonary disease can be avoided or lessened by stopping smoking, the risk of lung cancer remains a serious problem. I believe your uncle's doctors were correct in their assessment.

And in a related column published several months later, Dr. Gott responded to the question of birth control pills and smoking. Here's part of that column.

Smokes and Pill Bad Mix

DEAR DR. GOTT: I'm a 30-year-old female and have been on birth control pills since I was 18. I smoke a pack and a half to two packs of cigarettes per week. I'm concerned about all the reports I've read recently regarding birth control and cancer. What should I do?

DEAR READER: If you have an annual gynecological examination, including pap smears, I don't believe you have to worry about developing a problem with cancer from birth control pills. Reports linking the pill and breast cancer have been inconsistent in establishing a relationship between the two. I'm more concerned about blood clots. Several studies have shown that smokers who take oral contraceptives have a much higher incidence of blood clots in the leg veins (thrombophlebitis). These clots can migrate to the lungs (pulmonary embolism). Because of this dangerous consequence, many gynecologists refuse to prescribe birth control pills to women who smoke. I think you ought to get off the cigarettes.

I think we'd better call Doctor Brown and make sure this prescription says **<u>10,000</u>** Cigo-Ban pills !

Chapter 10

There's a growing tendency for medical doctors to tell their patients to butt out or find another doctor. Many of them don't want to waste their time treating smoking-related diseases, arguing that they try to treat these problems, but unless the patient quits smoking, it's a losing battle. Many smokers are not taking an active part in their own health care. For some patients, that ultimatum is all they needed. Many have quit smoking because they don't want to change doctors, or they realize that the warning makes sense. Even though this effective advice is for the ultimate good of the patients' health, legal beagles and smokers rights activists are claiming that doctors have no right to insist that their patients do anything to improve their health. The only patient a doctor can refuse treatment for is a habitual drug user. So what's the difference? Addiction is addiction, and if you're willfully destroying your body with drugs … OR tobacco, medical specialists should have the right to deny treatment. Besides, self-inflicted smoking-related illness drives up the cost of medical care, and uses up valuable time and space for illnesses that deserve the full attention of practitioners. If that isn't reason enough to kick the habit, think about your cat. That's right, second-hand smoke is killing pet cats by causing feline lymphoma, which kills 75% of its victims within 2 months.

Statistical studies have proven that second-hand smoke more than doubles the risk for kitties, and in a two-smoker home, the risk increases four times.

These studies even suggest that there may be an increased risk of lymphoma in children, however more definitive surveys are needed for proof. Veterinarians can identify cats and dogs whose owners smoke. The accumulation of smoke and side-stream by-products in their fur is amazing.

And it's amazing what some people will do for a puff. At the University of Arkansas a student decided to light up in his dorm, however since it was a smoke-free environment, he climbed out onto a fifth-floor ledge to enjoy his smoke. He died when he hit the ground.

Meanwhile, a Greyhound bus rolled over on the highway south of Phoenix, because a passenger who was frustrated because he wasn't allowed to smoke decided to fight with the driver. He wanted to take over the steering wheel and pull the bus off the road so he could light up. The bus was going 70 miles an hour. 33 people were injured.

Two elderly ladies were outside their nursing home, having a smoke, when it started to rain. One of the ladies pulled out a condom, cut off the end, put it over her cigarette.

Lady 1: "What's that?"

Lady 2: "A condom. Now my cigarette doesn't get wet."

Lady 1: "Where did you get it?"

Lady 2: "You can get them at any drugstore."

The next day, Lady 1 heads into the local drugstore and announces to the pharmacist that she wants a box of condoms. The guy, obviously embarrassed, looks at her kind of strangely (she is, after all, over 80 years of age), but very delicately asks what brand she prefers. Lady 1: "Doesn't matter son, as long as it fits a Camel."

The pharmacist fainted

Four worms were placed into four separate jars. The first worm was put into a jar of alcohol. The second worm was put into a jar of cigarette smoke. The third worm was put into a jar of sperm. The last worm was put into a jar of soil. After one day: First worm: dead. Second worm: dead. Third worm: dead. Fourth worm: alive. **Lesson:** As long as you drink, smoke and have sex, you won't get worms.

It says right here on the container.
"Do not use near open flame."

Chapter 11

Statistics can be boring. Here's one that's frightening. Four hundred and fifty five people is a good sized crowd. It would take that many folks to fill two good sized movie theaters. And that's how many ***women*** die **<u>EVERY DAY</u>** in the United States from smoking-related diseases. One woman dies from smoking ***every three and a half minutes*** in the U.S.A. It has become the leading killer of women in just two generations. And that number of deaths represents only 39% of the 400,000-plus deaths caused by smoking annually. Lung cancer kills 27,000 more women every year than breast cancer. And with one in five women smoking, and more teen-aged girls lighting up every year, those figures are on a frightening upward swing. Tobacco companies spent billions of dollars annually on ads targeting women. Young girls were lured into the habit by commercials featuring slim sexy girls with slogans saying "Until I find a real man, I'll take a real smoke"!! By taking that simple first puff, many young women were handed a death sentence. Quitting smoking significantly reduces the risks of weed-induced illnesses ... cancer, heart, lung and other diseases. But there are many other risks for female smokers, including menstrual irregularities, early menopause, osteoporosis or bone-thinning, cervical cancer, dangerous blood clots if they are using birth control pills, and of course arthritis. And to make matters worse, patches and nicotine gum are much less effective on women that they are on men. The smoking rate among men is decreasing more rapidly than in women. Men smoke because their systems are triggered by a need for nicotine. Women smoke because of the cues associated with their smoking behavior. They are hooked on the sensory effects of smoking … seeing and smelling tobacco smoke … the social pleasures involved --the smoking rituals. More attention must be paid to these triggers, and less to the 'treatments', such as gums and patches, although these devices are occasionally successful, but usually in men. Keeping thin is one of the false crutches women use to justify their smoking. This mistaken belief is a common thread in comments by women canvassed on their reasons for smoking. Learning new eating habits and seeking literature on how to quit smoking and stay slim can overcome this barrier to quitting. And quitting isn't usually a one-shot effort. Most ex-smokers tried to quit five times on average before they finally succeeded. Studies show that this process takes longer for women. Although the patch can be helpful in some cases, they are virtually useless when used by pregnant women. The theory is that pregnancy alters the way the nicotine is metabolized, therefore pregnant women don't find the patch helpful.

Another very popular aid to quitting the weed is the so-called electronic or e-cigarette. This popular electronic inhaler is also known as the PV or personal vaporizer and electronic nicotine delivery system, ENDS. They are designed to simulate the tactile action and sensory 'feel' of smoking an actual cigarette. Cleverly designed to look and feel like a 'real' cigarette, the unit contains a tiny heating element which vaporizes a flavored liquid. Some models actually release a small dose of nicotine as well. They are also available disguised as cigars. Studies are underway to determine the possible negative health implications of these devices, however they are probably less damaging than tobacco products. Although there is no actual smoke involved in their use, there are restrictions on them in some areas. The debate continues, with some studies claiming that there is no proof that e-cigarettes are beneficial, while others support their use as effective aids to quitting smoking. Still other studies conclude that a strong regulatory system for e-cigarette distribution is needed until their safety and efficacy are proven. But if they work for you, and if they effectively satisfy the craving for a cigarette 'fix', they might be worth a try -- unless they are otherwise proven to be unhealthy.

The biggest single cause of teen-age smoking is peer-pressure. It only takes a couple of weeks for a young girl … or boy … to become hooked, although the analysis showed that it takes slightly longer for boys to become addicted. It can even happen after just one smoke! So studies have proven that addiction ***can*** take place with the very first cigarette. Earlier tests indicated that teenagers didn't consider themselves addicted unless they smoked 10 to 20 cigarettes a day. Now most of them feel hooked even though they smoke two a day. Symptoms include a craving for a cigarette, or an inability to concentrate when it isn't possible to have a cigarette. Proof of the strength of the addiction is the statistic which shows that students who exhibited signs of addiction were 30 times less likely to succeed in any attempt to quit smoking. The study revealed that because the teen-aged brain is still developing, Adolescents are more likely to develop an addiction to smoking. Smokers who start at an early age also have the greatest trouble quitting as adults, and develop into heavier smokers as they get older. That's why it's vital to get the message across to young smokers early. If it can prevent COPD (Chronic Obstructive Pulmonary Disease) in later years, it's worth mentioning this deadly condition yet again. Cigarette smoking and air pollution have led to a dramatic rise in the numbers of people suffering from chronic lung disease, or COPD. COPD results in the destruction of the delicate air sacs (alveoli) which allow the lungs to get rid of carbon dioxide and absorb oxygen from the air we breathe. COPD is also associated with Asthma and pulmonary scarring. Early stages of COPD are marked by slight intolerance to exercise, and occasional breathlessness. Smoking definitely aggravates this condition. Eventually the sufferer experiences shortness of breath, over-expanded chest, difficulty in breathing while at rest, cough and general weakness. As the condition evolves into the terminal stages, patients slowly suffocate. An enormous amount of energy is expended with each breath, often accompanied by oxygen supplements. Amazingly, many sufferers from COPD continue to smoke!

A major newspaper once ran a limerick contest on the subject of smoking/quitting smoking. Here were the three entries I submitted.

Surrounded by ashes and smoke,
And a cough that is more like a choke,
The smoker still thinks
That the smoking ban stinks.
But it's him, and he will 'til he croaks.

– – – – – – – –

Smoking is lovely they say.
I go through two packs a day.
This pain in my chest,
My bad breath, and the rest
Of my problems may soon go away.
(When there in my casket I lay!)

– – – – – –

Shove dried weed in a long paper tube,
Light the end and suck smoke with exube…
Rance: so underrated,
And so-phosticated …
Believe that, and you're REALLY a boob.

Alas, none of these limericks won!

Long flight ?

We've all heard the old wives' tale that "It's harder for women to quit smoking than it is for men." Well get ready for a surprise. It ***IS*** harder for women to quit smoking according to recent studies conducted by U.S. medical schools. The studies also discovered that patches and nicotine gum products are not as effective for women. The analysis also showed that although there is a reduction in smoking generally, it is not decreasing as rapidly among women. This fact is worth repeating. Addiction in men is predominately based on a chemical dependency. In women, the habit is triggered by "environmental cues". Women are hooked on the tactile and visual effects of smoking, or the social acceptability and pleasures involved in the ritual surrounding smoking. The researchers concluded that the focus should be on treating smokers to recognize and deal with those cues. One of the subliminal motives for smoking among women is the belief that they can stay thin because of the appetite suppressants in cigarettes. Both men and women average five attempts to quit smoking before they actually succeed, however it's a significantly longer process for women. Pregnant women who try to quit smoking using the patch might as well save their money, according to the study. Pregnant women declare that the patch is useless, probably because they metabolize nicotine differently than men do. Proof that smoking is equally deadly for both genders lies in Canadian statistics that show 7,400 Canadian women will die of lung cancer in the current year, and 5,500 will die of breast cancer. In spite of these alarming statistics, a report issued by the U.S. Surgeon General's office claims that smoking related illnesses among American women are rapidly reaching epidemic proportions. 165,000 women die each year from diseases linked to smoking, which means that it has become the leading cause of premature death in women in just two generations. The tobacco industry promotes its product by spending nearly $1 million *every hour.* There are over 400,000 smoking related deaths in the U.S. each year, and 39 percent of those victims are women. That's over twice as many as there were in 1965. I mentioned this statistic a few pages back. It's worth repeating. Every three and a half minutes, another woman dies as a result of smoking. Women are rightly concerned about the number of deaths from breast cancer annually, but many do not realize that lung cancer is now the number one cancer killer among women. 27,000 more women will die from lung cancer than breast cancer this year. Although the ratio of women smokers remains at about one in five, 30 percent more teenage girls are smoking now than there were a decade ago. The national goal of cutting smoking by women in half in the next ten years will be almost impossible to achieve, when the industry spends over eight billion dollars a year in advertising. Ads that feature ultra-thin women lure young girls to the habit, and opponents to this brand of advertising claim that "what starts out as a simple puff can lead to a death sentence." Previous attempts by Federal government agencies to combat the lure of advertising failed in a Supreme Court challenge. Young women are ignoring the fact that quitting the habit significantly reduces the chance of smoking related diseases… cancer and heart and lung disease. Let me repeat this fact. Female smokers also face additional risks such as menstrual irregularities, early menopause, infertility, loss of bone density, osteoporosis, arthritis, cervical cancer, and the possibility of dangerous blood clots if they smoke while on birth control pills.

Chapter 12

I don't know anyone who has been able to quit smoking completely on the very first try. There are just too many temptations out there, and we all know that it's not easy. However if you have managed to stay off the weed for a few days or weeks and suddenly have a relapse, don't be embarrassed or ashamed. Most successful 'quitters' only got there after several attempts. Most relapses happen within the first week, or often the first three months after quitting. These relapses are triggered by situations you used to associate with smoking… like stress…or when enjoying a drink. Knowing that these situations can be challenging can help you prepare for them, or perhaps avoid them. And support from friends and family is crucial. And don't forget to reward yourself for your effort. It doesn't take long for the money saved by not buying smokes to add up to a nice treat, or even an exotic holiday. If a friend or family member is thinking about quitting, here are a few things that **DON'T** work:

- Lectures or preaching about the health hazards. (Most smokers believe they have "heard it all".)
- Nagging - (Definitely a no-no)
- Ultimatums - ("If you don't quit, we're through.")

- Put-downs - (Destroy the incentive.)
- Guilt-trips - Do not make smokers feel guilty about smoking. Offer support, not blame.

Smoking is a powerful addiction for many smokers, and quitting can be painfully difficult. For some, smoking has helped them concentrate, deal with stress, relax and cope with boredom. Each smoker has their own reasons for smoking. Some have no idea why they smoke. Each person will seek their own motivation for quitting. Some will never be motivated enough to quit. Quitting smoking isn't just about "stopping" smoking, it means changing how you think and feel about smoking. Each smoker has to find their own time to quit, and work their way through it at their own speed and in their own way. Every quitting experience is different. For many, quitting the habit will be the most difficult thing they will ever do. Others will not find it hard. There are actually five stages a smoker goes through on the way to becoming a non-smoker:

1. Not thinking about quitting
2. Thinking about quitting, but not ready to quit
3. Getting ready to quit
4. Quitting
5. Remaining a non-smoker.

If your friend or family member is trying to quit, and you are a confirmed smoker, you can still help in many ways:

- Keep in mind that while your friend no longer wants to smoke, they do still want to be your friend.
- You don't have to quit, but you can help your friend to quit.
- Don't make fun of their preparations or their quit attempts. Support them even if it causes you some inconvenience.
- Help out by not smoking at certain times and places. Ask your friend what would be most helpful.
- Don't offer cigarettes, or do anything else to encourage them to start smoking again. Let them make their own choice.

And if they fall off the wagon, don't nag. Let them know you understand that quitting is not easy, and that most people make two or three attempts before succeeding. Encourage them to keep trying at their own speed.

Here are a few additional reasons why you might want to consider quitting smoking. Recent studies at Montreal's McGill University show that smoking also causes tumors of the mouth, tongue, throat and lips. It also leads to a build up of cancer-causing agents in the bladder, pancreas, cervix, rectum and genitalia. These agents can promote the development of the disease because it increases the capacity of cells to absorb and carry cancer-causing agents. And if you smoke and drink, you overwhelmingly increase risks.

The Surgeon-General has called smoking the most important of the known modifiable risk factors for coronary heart disease in the U.S.

Back in 1968 my good pal Dave Brown was already considered to be a significant columnist and journalist. His preeminence as an investigative journalist, senior editor and featured columnist continues today. When I asked him about his smoking addiction, he told me that back in 1968 he had decided to kick the habit, and to reinforce the decision, he wrote a column about it. He figured that by doing so it would be almost impossible to back down on his commitment. At about that time the Federal government decided it was time to alert the Canadian public to the dangers of smoking. They began the process of publishing a small book entitled "How We Quit Smoking". It featured brief essays from prominent Canadians on the subject, and Dave Brown was one of the contributors. (By the way, the book was sent to me by another very good friend, Sidney Ledson, who happened to be the illustrator of the book. His name isn't mentioned anywhere in the credits !) Meanwhile, Dave wrote his essay for this inspirational little publication and sent it to the federal government employee in charge of the project. About two years later the book was released. Here's the last paragraph of Dave's contribution: "I know people who quit for as long as five years, and started again. I hope I'm not one of those. Freedom from the smoking habit can only be felt when you know you've got it beat. It's a great feeling. Dave Brown."

When I mentioned to Dave that I had found this little essay, he laughed. "It took them a couple of years to produce that book. Six months before it was released, I was smoking again.

Knowing my senior daughter Susan as well as I do (over 40 years!) I wouldn't be surprised if she had started smoking when she was four years old. She still smokes, however she restricts her habit to the great outdoors. She is now the only member of the family addicted to the weed. The first time I ever saw Susan smoking became a memorable event. We lived in a garden home in Ottawa's west end, and there were a number of kids in their early teens growing up in the neighborhood. One of their favorite hang-outs was a nearby Oriental restaurant. One evening my wife and I had run out of cigarettes, so I wandered over to the restaurant to pick up a pack. As soon as I entered the place, I spotted my 14-year-old daughter being her usual 'life-of-the-party', standing beside one of the booths which was crammed with teen-agers. All of them were smoking like fiends, the way teens do when they first get into the habit. Susan was busy gabbing away and didn't notice my arrival. As I watched her, she took an enormous drag on her cigarette, and at that exact moment she spotted me looking at her. The cigarette somehow disappeared. It wound up on the floor where she deftly ground it under her shoe. Meanwhile the enormous drag was still somewhere deep inside her lungs....where it stayed for a re-e-e-eally long time, because I kept looking at her, waiting for the tell-tale smoke to exit. Finally she couldn't hold her frozen grin or her breath any longer, and just as the smoke was about to come out of her ears, she exhaled and went into a coughing fit. In those days if your kids smoked, you didn't go into a rage… you merely accepted it as a part of 'growing up.' Now we know better. Susan has tried everything … the patch, cold turkey, nicotine gum, and nothing works for her. Maybe someday the light will go on and she'll quit. Then again, maybe not!

Chapter 13

Have you ever seen anything more 'cowboy macho' that the way John Wayne could roll a cigarette … ***with one hand*** ? Yessirree, ol' John could twist a makin's roll-yer-own with a Vogue paper and a bag of Turrets Fine-Cut, and at the same time intimidate the local bad guy into gettin' outa Dodge City. It took me a long time to learn how to roll my own cigarettes, and believe me, it took both hands. Sometimes it actually looked like a cigarette. Most of the time it looked like a lumpy piece of toilet paper with shredded wheat hanging out the end. In those days even though smokes only cost twenty-five cents a pack, it was still expensive, because the average wage was about twenty-five cents an hour. So a tin of tobacco and a package of papers would yield about four times as many weeds at the same cost as one pack of 'tailor-mades.' For awhile we owned a cigarette rolling machine. It was a neat rig that produced three cigarettes at a time … all in one piece. The papers were about fourteen inches long. You placed a paper (sticky-side out) in the groove formed by a piece of rubberized cloth. Then you filled the paper with a neat line of tobacco, (some people actually put other stuff in there too !) Then you would lick the gummed edge of the paper, and by sliding the front edge of the machine under a barrier, somehow a very long cigarette was formed. Unless you wanted to smoke a very king-sized cigarette, you would then place it in a marked groove and slice it into regulation-sized cigarettes with a razor-blade. This device would produce two normal sized weeds and one slightly longer. For some reason I always trimmed that extra little bit off. It never dawned on me that I could have had one king-sized cigarette for every two normal ones. In later years there were machines that would enable you to make your own filter-tip cigarettes, which looked just like real tailor-mades. Most people carried their home made weeds is plastic containers. If you wanted to look sophisticated and pretend you could afford 'real' cigarettes, you would pick up an empty brand-name package and insert your el-cheapos. The trend to 'repackage' your smokes seems to be coming back. With graphic pictures and warnings on most packages now, many folks are covering up those warnings with counterfeit covers, hand designed inserts, and even crocheted pouches to carry their weeds around in.

And then there's *SECOND-HAND* smoke. If you think smoking is bad, wait 'til you hear what happens when you live with or work near a smoker. Second-hand smoke is the most common and harmful form of indoor air pollution. Smokers fill the air with two kinds of smoke.

Mainstream: Smoke that is first inhaled then exhaled by the smoker.

Side-stream: Smoke that goes directly into the air from the burning end of the cigarette between puffs.

Second-hand smoke has up to 4,000 chemicals in it!

Chemical tests found that side-stream smoke has more tar, nicotine and other cancer-causing chemicals than main-stream smoke. In fact there are three cancer-causing chemicals in second-hand smoke that are so dangerous, the North American air quality rules used by most governments insist that no one should ***ever*** be exposed to them ! 85% of the smoke from a cigarette is side-stream. Smokers already know the probable effect smoking will have on their health. However many don't realize that their smoke affects the health of the people around them.

Innocent bystanders … many of them children suffer from:

- eye irritation
- headache
- nasal discomfort and sneezing
- cough and sore throat
- nausea and dizziness
- increased heart rate and blood pressure

And for the 25% of the population suffering from asthma, angina or allergies, second-hand smoke leads to:

- Reduced ability to take in and use oxygen
- Heart disease and lung cancer in non-smokers

- The death of nearly 4,000 Canadian and American non-smokers from lung cancer.

Employers pay a big price for smoking employees. It has been estimated that each smoker costs the employers more than $2,000 per year because of:

- Increased absenteeism
- Decreased productivity
- Increased insurance premiums
- Increased property damage
- Costs from non-smokers' exposure to second-hand smoke.

Amazingly, nicotine can be found in the blood of non-smokers from 2 to 40 hours after exposure to second-hand smoke. Normal ventilation in homes isn't able to remove all of the cancer-causing chemicals and gasses found in second-hand smoke. So if you're a smoker, why not do your family a favor and smoke outside the home. At work, smoke only in specially vented areas.

Did you put your pipe in
your pocket again ?

Chapter 14

WHAT'S IN THAT CIGARETTE BUTT ?

Carbon monoxide: the fumes that come from your car;
Formaldehyde: used to preserve corpses;
Ammonia: a bathroom and kitchen cleaner;
Carbon dioxide: helps deplete the ozone layer;
plus metals: copper, mercury, lead, zinc and aluminum.

In the U.S. 400,000 Americans die every year because of health problems due to smoking. 1 out of every 6 deaths each year is related to smoking.

Age and education demographics show that those with:

9 - 11 years of education	37.4% smoke
16 years of education	11.6% smoke
Below the poverty level	33.3% smoke
Psychiatric outpatients	50% smoke
Schizophrenic patients	90% smoke
Manic-depressive patients	70% smoke
Alcoholics	90% smoke

Marijuana contains higher concentrations of cancer-causing components than tobacco. Smoking five 'joints' a week has the same risk as smoking a full package of cigarettes a day!! It can also cause early fetus abortion in pregnancy.

Babies born to marijuana users were shorter, weighed less had smaller head sizes, and had features resembling fetal alcohol syndrome, than those born to mothers who did not use the drug.

Animal and human studies show that marijuana impairs the ability of T-cells in the lungs' immune defense system to fight off some infections. People with HIV and others whose immune system is impaired should avoid marijuana use.

Marijuana produces a great risk of getting lung infections such as pneumonia. Continued marijuana use can lead to abnormal functions of lungs and airways. Scientists have found signs of lung tissue injured or destroyed by marijuana smoke.

It is not only possible but very likely that users will become addicted to marijuana, and increased intake of THC, a component of marijuana, can increase the risk of certain mental illnesses such as schizophrenia.

Now to add to the lure of smoking, there's a new kind of cigarette out there that targets teens. They're called **bidi.**

Teenagers think they're cool because they come from India, look like a marijuana joint … and they're flavored! The kids think they're harmless, but in fact they are more dangerous than conventional cigarettes. Many teens switch to bidis because they think they aren't real cigarettes, but these strange looking weeds actually contain three times the nicotine concentration of North American cigarettes. And to add to the problem, the leaf used to wrap these insidious smokes is non-porous and doesn't allow the same mix of air and smoke as conventional cigarettes. What next??

Cigarette smoking contributes to higher incidence of head and neck cancer in some smokers.

Chapter 15

In December pharmacists always stock up on patches and pills to help people quit smoking, because New Years is the most popular and logical time to swear off. Surveys indicate that over 70% of smokers would like to quit, and in the week before and after January 1st, they swarm in droves to the drug stores for products that will help them with their decision. Unfortunately only a small percentage of them manage to stay off the habit. By February the sale of these products is back to normal. Many swear off as a first step towards a healthy life-style. Others are concerned that they might not be around to see their children grow up.

When the time comes to quit smoking, the idea of cold turkey is not an option for most people. There are numerous options out there to help us through the difficult post-weed period. It's always wise to confer with your doctor before deciding on a treatment.

Acupuncture: The ear is the target, and the treatment results in creating a very bitter taste in the mouth reminiscent of strong cigarette smoke. This reduces the desire to smoke, and after two or three treatments and a little applied will power, there is a relatively high success rate. If you are a heavy smoker, you will need more treatments.

Herbal Remedies: Lobelia is a non-addictive herbal ingredient which can be administered by capsule or spray. It tricks your body into thinking that you are having a cigarette, and it reduces withdrawal symptoms. This gives the body time to get rid of toxins and nicotine.

Hypnosis: Hypnosis works on the theory that cravings, habits and desires are controlled by the subconscious mind. Hypnosis allegedly reprograms the subconscious to allow the conscious mind to concentrate on quitting smoking without interference. It is supposed to strengthen motivation and will-power.

Nicotine gum: The user regulates the dosage of these smoking suppressants, however the gum itself can become addictive. In addition certain acidic foods such as tomatoes or orange drinks should be avoided because of their interference with nicotine absorption. No food or drink for at least fifteen minutes before chewing.

Quitting smoking is hardest when the smoker is faced with day to day situations which act as triggers to the desire for a weed. The most difficult situation is the leisurely visit to the pub. A couple of beers, a snack, and voila. Where did that cigarette come from?

There are two fundamental reasons why people smoke:

1. Your system very quickly learns to crave nicotine;
2. The smoking habit is triggered by association with certain activities, situations and occasions.

When you quit the weed, it takes your body several days to adjust to the change. You feel light-headed and sort of 'out of it'. These symptoms are known as 'withdrawal' and can include changes in body temperature, digestion, heart-rate, appetite and muscle tone. Many people may even experience anxiety and for some it will mean irritability and disturbed sleep. These reactions are not shared by everyone who quits smoking. Often the withdrawal symptoms are linked to the degree of addiction. Many smokers claim that they have legitimate reasons for smoking which include controlling anger, coping with stress, peer pressure from family and associates, and concern about gaining weight if they quit smoking. Although many people can quit cold-turkey, most smokers need to be educated and prepared for the onslaught of emotional, physical and psychological obstacles they will face. Your family doctor or pharmacist can help you with advice and encouragement and give you practical coping strategies and skills to help you through the first difficult days. Some pharmaceutical chains support national 'Stop Smoking' campaigns to help make that decision a bit easier. The Canadian Cancer Society asks you to answer four simple questions to help determine your degree of addiction. Answer yes or no to the following questions.

1. I smoke on average more than 10 cigarettes each day.
2. I usually smoke within 30 minutes of waking up in the morning.
3. I find it difficult to go for more than four hours without smoking.
4. When I try to quit or cut back on the amount I smoke, I experience irritability, difficulty concentrating, trouble sleeping, dizziness, frustration and changes in my appetite.

People with a low level of addiction will answer NO to all of these questions. This category of smoker will be able to quit by concentrating on what influences your desire to smoke.

If you answered YES to one or two of these questions, you are probably moderately addicted to smoking and may need medical treatment to help you quit.

If you answered YES to three or more of these questions, you are probably highly addicted to nicotine. Quitting will require a combination of a smoking cessation program and medical treatment for nicotine addiction.

And it ***IS*** addictive. By incorporating itself into the brain's chemical processes and functions, it becomes psychoactive. The 'habit' imprints itself into the fabric of our daily lives and becomes associated with everything from pleasure, anxiety, stress, food, sex, virtually all of our fundamental forces.

So there you have it.

You have to ***want*** to quit.

When you realize that nicotine is one of the most addictive substances in existence … even more addictive than heroin … you can begin to appreciate how easy it is to become addicted and how difficult it can be to quit.

There are many suggestions to help the smoker through the process of ending the smoking routine/ lifestyle. It seems an oversimplification, but replacing cigarettes with carrot or celery sticks is often a very successful replacement therapy which mimics the act of holding a cigarette.

Setting a pre-determined 'stopping-date' is often a very useful tool. By focusing on a birthday or special event as a target for quitting, smokers can often build up to the actual moment of butting out for the last time, and provide an anniversary moment which will enable them to reinforce their decision. Every smoker must create his or her own formula for quitting. With a resolute plan and firm motivation, you can be one of the fifty to sixty percent of smokers who are able to quit the habit for good. It takes a lot of time and effort, but it will make a huge difference in your quality of life and in the number of years you will be around to enjoy it.

Good luck!

I wonder if those smokers over there realize how bad it is for them.

About the Author

In spite of being born in a log cabin in South Porcupine Ontario at the beginning of the Gtreat Depression, (there is no North Porcupine!) Ray Stone never became President of anything. Well actually he is Past President of the National Press Club of Canada, and President/ founder of C.R.A.P., the Committee for the removal of Artistic Pollution.

This fact will cause further angst among the political correctoids who are forewarned not to read this book. His school and street education in Windsor Ontario has given him a rather warped view of society, and in particular, the vehicularly challenged among us. He survived a decade or so in the RCAF (Post-war) including a brief stint with NATO in Europe and two years as a Public Relations Officer at a NORAD base in Northern Michigan. Following his voluntary release from the Air Force, he worked for the CBC as a 'talking head' before returning to Ottawa to work as a Special Assistant to several Cabinet Ministers. He rounded out his career with the Public Service as Head of the film, video and exhibits division of

Transport Canada Public Affairs, and as a Major in the Air Force Reserves. Since retiring from the 'Feds', he has free-lanced for the Canadian Broadcasting Corporation, acted in several films, hosted a variety of television series, including the award-winning "To Your Health" and for fifteen years was moderator of a phone-in radio show "Experts On Call" on News-Talk Radio, 580-CFRA in Ottawa. His first book, **"Women Can't Merge, Men Won't Yield"** is an equal opportunity rant against stupid male drivers and oblivious female drivers.

www.ingramcontent.com/pod-product-compliance
Ingram Content Group UK Ltd.
Pitfield, Milton Keynes, MK11 3LW, UK
UKHW041928190726
13854UKWH00004B/1503

9 781483 405247